T0304471

NERVE CURRICULUM

FUTUREPOEM BOOKS
NEW YORK CITY
2023

.

NERVE CURRICULUM

Manuel Paul López

first edition | first printing

This edition first published in paperback by Futurepoem
P.O. Box 7687 JAF Station
NY, NY 10116
www.futurepoem.com

Executive Editor: Dan Machlin
Managing Editors: Aiden Farrell, Carly Dashiell
Guest Editors: Rosa Alcalá, Marie Buck, and Farnoosh Fathi
Cover design: Everything Studio (www.everythingstudio.com)
Interior design: HR Hegnauer (www.hrhegnauer.com)
Copy editor: Marcella Durand
Typefaces: Arno Pro
Printed in the United States of America on acid-free paper

This project is supported by awards from the National Endowment for the Arts, the New York State Council on the Arts with the support of Governor Kathy Hochul and the New York State Legislature, and by public funds from the New York City Department of Cultural Affairs in partnership with the City Council. Futurepoem is also supported by our individual donors, subscribers, and readers, The Literary Arts Emergency Fund, Tamaas, Leslie Scalapino Fund, New York Community Trust, and Leaves of Grass Fund. Futurepoem Inc. is a New York state-based 501(c)3 non-profit organization dedicated to creating a greater public awareness and appreciation of innovative literature.

Distributed to the trade by Small Press Distribution, Berkeley, California
Toll-free number (U.S. only): 800.869.7553
Bay Area/International: 510.524.1668
orders@spdbooks.org
www.spdbooks.org

CONTENTS

FOUR

FIVE

for mandie nicole

Los Copetes

My plastic gun couldn't save us   Those plastic guns couldn't save our

1980s copetes   We all had them   I carried my plastic black uzi

replica to Rafa's every Saturday at 6 p.m.   Asked his ma   *señora*

Alvarado   is Rafa home   Hola Turi   let me call him   Would you

like something to drink   No thank you señora   Rafa   Turi's here

Your twelve gauge is in the laundry basket   está debajo de tus calzones

hediondos   Me oíste   Next time you better behave   Ay amá   Me

oíste   Boom you're dead   My primo Tortuga brought the Pirates of

the Caribbean musket his stepdad bought for his ass at Disneyland when

Dennis first dated my tía   *¡bribe of all bribes!*   their first "family

vacation"   that little weasel   We laughed at that long skinny thing

that lumber and pipe   O silly cap gun   tricks are for kids   We

called him one-shot Tortuga   *Ah fuck you* Tortuga blasted   Too

bad he never saw the twelve crosshairs dancing across his forehead like

a small swarm of chicharras   That pirata long arm was the unlucky

draw   last gat picked from the pile   too slow for combat   poor

relic of another era   We brought rapid-fire burners and injured

ourselves in the mulberries that kicked and scratched when we hid from each other   hunters of the bush   *Shut up Beto they're gonna hear*

you   Why do you always have to sound like some pinche porn star huffing

like that   Where's your asthma pump Stupid   I don't want to carry your

ass home again   Though we all eventually arrived home bleeding and

scratching   Max nearly suffocated when he hid in Rafa's abandoned

icebox one necro summer when he stiffened up in the heat of battle afraid

to face the massacre that kaboomed in Matthew's front yard   bodies

like desiccated tree bark   small ribbons of commemoration we were

when our likenesses escaped above rooftops upon our corporeal deaths

musty adolescent release   each week the gang of us like second-hand

cigarette smoke we floated past the Jack in the Box sign on Fourth Street

We cried *Boom you're dead* when we pulled the trigger and dutifully

fell   what commitment to death   such ashy allegiance we screamed

when we won   small bodies strewn across the lawns of a small desert

town   We brought our guns and figured two solid hours of fun enough

before our mothers cried bathwater out open kitchen windows   *Boom*

you're dead Sylvio whispered into my ear as I squatted behind Leo's dad's

'82 Camaro my pirate musket (I was the last to draw) trained on Tortuga's

neck   What dread when fear squirrels up and screeches from the bottom

of a travieso's throat   Then BAM   the great fat cranial sneeze   all

out   our blood-hued mucus   our nickelodeon civil war   our imagined transcendence   We brought our guns loyal to death and fell

while Darlene's mom's favorite rose bush periscoped earth with its roots

and searched for Sergio's bones cancered one year before   Fire ants

that memorialized Saturday's tennis shoe pile with their electric soil music

canvas pyre   rescue party   wicked deforestation   skeletal loggers

My branches arrived broken and dry   a stiff abomination left to wither

on my parents' front porch   small heap of me pleading bath time to rinse

away the agony of that rogue astilla that somehow lodged its wicked prick

into my tiny heel   needlepoint to my birth balloon   explosion of the

day's prayer that once promised our future arrivals unharmed

after PJ Harvey's "In the Dark Places"

ONE

In the open mouth of grief there is a candle
—Jack Hirschman

Nerve Curriculum

I arrived greeted by a team of two-bit hustlers:

doctors,
administrators,
phlebotomists,
nurses,
officers of the state.

The welcome committee attended my birth and infuriated my first public breath.

A real clown car. I swear the driver was drunk!

Tongues clucked to the rhythms of my newborn bubble guts.
Dank eupnea that fumigated my first exhibition with a flatulent grief.

Nonetheless, I thanked them for embracing me into the great soggy meat parade.

They nodded. Then engaged in a round of spirited debates about the
possibilities of a state-sanctioned self.

Where's my script, I demanded. What character will I play, I screamed,
before they shoved a roll of wet paper towels into my mouth, hooting and
hollering, laughing at me, all while promising the eternal shush.

Play

#ROOKIEOFTHEYEAR!: Do you know what it feels like to possess a glass object beneath your chest that is on the verge of constant breakage? No eyes saw my fragility incarnate. There were moments when I needed to simply sit myself on the pitcher's mound and cry. But I didn't. Much to my detriment. You ask the cocaine? The cocaine replies: *Cocaine is. Cocaine is all EYE.*

THE ROSIN BAG: Uh Huh, Uh Huh—O, #ROOKIEOFTHEYEAR!, please continue this tale.

#ROOKIEOFTHEYEAR!: And so it was an ice cube that sat just beneath the umpire's skull. Always melting. My work was a race against that melting. I missed the World Series parade. Millions of people waited. And I'm still picking up the stepped-on ticker tape and the faded confetti everywhere I go.

THE ROSIN BAG: I knew you. You were the great one. As I graced your hand I embarked upon space travel.

#ROOKIEOFTHEYEAR!: My hands?—

THE ROSIN BAG: Your hand.

#ROOKIEOFTHEYEAR!: I was vilified by the media.

THE ROSIN BAG: So!

#ROOKIEOFTHEYEAR!: So my mother and father bore the shame!

THE ROSIN BAG: And now that media bears the shame. You were a meteorite that flew over Manhattan. You keep flying *over* Manhattan. I scrawled your name in dirt beneath me and waited patiently for the next though I knew the next would never come. There's only one—

#ROOKIEOFTHEYEAR!: 19 Ks.

THE ROSIN BAG: 20-plus game winner. Cy Young. Rookie PRINCE!

#ROOKIEOFTHEYEAR!: Let's write a new script and forget!

THE ROSIN BAG: From your hand I reached someone's heaven.

#ROOKIEOFTHEYEAR!: I'm a candle that won't blow out.

THE ROSIN BAG: O hush and heal. None of this is for real.

Pillow Talk

In high school, gagger meant methamphetamine:

Got any gagger? / Got any gagger? / Got any gagger?

In high school, we called small piles of glassy meth shavings wrapped in Kleenex ::: pillows.

We placed them on our tongues to avoid the excruciating nasal fry that threatened to rocket ship straight out the tops of our motherfucking heads if we snorted.

O, cute, dime-store plutonium trinkets
Gewgaw explosives.
Dear Ice Yellow Maximus.
Detonation powder.

My brain was a 24-hour convenience store.

The gagged never sleep.

The gagged wander waywardly through the corridors of the glass metropolis called More.

Fistfuls of household disinfectants seesawed my guts. I coughed up the sharp stench of Clorox.

I scrubbed sunshine from my stiff lash as if acidic and drove a jeep straight through my family's 24-hour roadblocks.

1. My breath disinfected my redheaded high school principal's comb over.
2. My breath ate the rusty hinges off the public bathroom doors adjacent to the junior varsity baseball field.
3. My breath eagle-eyed sleep like a jealous snoop donning green construction gloves, a trench coat, and a pair of pliers.
4. My breath bleached the meth-howl of masturbation.
5. My breath pounded three tombstones through my childhood skull.

In high school gagger meant methamphetamine.

In high school I was a numbers man who flunked physics when I blew glass through my nose.

In high school, we called small piles of glassy meth shavings wrapped in Kleenex ::: pillows.

Town, Town (Poem For 12 Voices)

There are infantile towns, juvenile towns, adolescent towns,
early mature towns, and mature towns. However, there are
also small "cities" that crouch at an infantile town's feet and
admit: Can we be towns too?

—A riff on a Wikipedia entry

"A hotel is where when you go there they have to let you in
If a room is available and you can convince them you can pay."

—Kenneth Koch

The grocery store is where you go when you need food to eat. Be sure to take your coupons, especially double-value coupons, because they can chew up your receipts like a swarm of termites. All of you will leave the market with wide, silly grins, the termites included, because they love the smell of your dinner table and will certainly die for the taste of a cutting board. Reward them, for they'll always be good to you, munching away at the profiteering hands that promise to rub your bone into chalk dust.

A minister's home is where you go when you're bound by doubt and the trees sway and whisper conspiracies, and the town's square squeaks with each step you take while everyone shushes before you arrive until just after you leave, only to chat again, and cheat, and distort, and explain how much you've grown into such a beguiling mongoose. With clasped hands they'll all nod in agreement. And then "Wow," the wind will say, "just wow," as it blows beneath their bedsheets and through their dirty dreams of dust devils dancing on your grave.

The post office is where you go when you need to deliver a letter or a bill. Drop your delivery into the blue steel receptacle, and say thank you as your tiny package burrows through the cold tile floor and inches across five states to pay its debt, or to say hello again, I miss you, to keep the spores of loneliness from once again flowering upon your door.

And the funeral parlor is where you go when you no longer feel like getting up to reintroduce yourself to the sun. Sing to the mortician's song, to the formal and proper prep. Celebrate the wooden vessel that will protect you on your extraterrestrial flight, your pine box music traversing intergalactic zip codes, stars that will polish each plank and plume.

A school is where you go when you'd like to rhyme words and add numbers, where little ones memorize errant patriotism, dream logic, and laughter before it all drains down the bathroom sink alongside a greying, itchy beard trim that looks like one million diminutive subtraction signs.

A gas station is where you go when your vehicle needs fuel or when you'd like sunflower seeds for the road. Tall lights reach over the hill. Looming signs with numbers explain delirious fuel fluctuations. Gas stations, quick stops caught between the fear and ecstasy of realizing you nearly found yourself stranded between a planet and a moon past midnight, a hedgehog, and a riverboat.

A fire department is a place you go if you'd like to slide down a brass pole. Ask the captain if it's OK then climb the stairs either way—permission is irrelevant now. In position, scream here we go! And twist and twirl on your descent as you slide through multiple floors waving, screaming the only fires today will be in our hearts! Sliding and sliding through thick layers of geologic rock until you suddenly find yourself in bed waking from your sleep with strange dust on your elbows.

A library is where you go when you need a book, when a book is necessary. Scan them, your book, your library card, and then nod or wink confidently at the librarian—that book belongs to you, at least momentarily, three weeks or so would be a guess. And if you choose, you can renew it and promise yourself to read it again and again like the first time you heard that strange voice in your head living a distant century ago near an ancient river that smelled of musk and rye.

A river is where you go when you'd like to wash your clothes or fish or create a reflection of yourself in the passing water with an airplane overhead, small hands waving from oval windows like tiny glass chandelier pendants offering light. A river is a current, an EKG reading that shares its news and then is done but somehow one feels reframed again like a portrait of yourself suspended above the earth.

A panadería is where you go because your heart is like bread and there's nothing more fabulous than visiting familia. Gracefully, the man and woman stand behind the counter, smiling as they always do, as they point to a row of pan dulce, bolillos and empanadas. Like a theater of shortening, the onlookers listen to your heart's beat and throb with sugary love, an offering of endless conchas and cochinitos dizzy with daydreams of beach sand and sea.

The police department is where you go when you need to put your head down on a desk and reflect about where we've come, where we're headed. When suddenly, the idea arrives, to take the controls from the dispatcher for one last announcement, to close your eyes and claim: *Calling all units, calling all units, today is the day you all leave us alone for good!*

A town's town is where one inscribes love for others with their fingertips and "I lived here once" in freshly poured concrete that will someday become porches and patios and sidewalks that together host the chatter of lives so far from considering losses mounting like poker chips drained of value and further occupation.

The Screwball Sleep

CRUSHED ICE IN GATORADE COOLER: I melt with you in me.

GATORADE: Not for not. These brutes imbibe like drought-beaten hillsides in the rain.

BAG OF SUNFLOWER SEEDS: I am one of the only entities, methinks, that can double in size once removed and ingested.

CRUSHED ICE IN GATORADE COOLER: We are strengths varied in our ways.

FERNANDO VALENZUELA: My screwball can erase the dreams of giants.

GATORADE: We've always considered you a savant, Fernando. For the dreams of giants often remain nightmares for those in their wake.

CRUSHED ICE IN GATORADE COOLER: This is true. Fernando, your admission melts me unto you.

GATORADE: To Fernando!

BAG OF SUNFLOWER SEEDS: To Fernando!

CRUSHED ICE IN GATORADE COOLER: To Fernando!

FERNANDO VALENZUELA: Bueno pues, now let us melt to the sound of a screwball sleep: *Ommmm.*

New World Gag (Dis)Order

I walked straight into the war cabinet's office and demanded all gaggers to put their hands in the air. This is a citizen's arrest, motherfuckers! I was a real Charles Bronson.

The room was empty and a vast stillness surrounded me like a bunch of slow motherfuckers who'd just got caught in a game of freeze tag. Up with those arms! Ya basta con las armas, but nobody, nobody.

Before I left, I heard the sound of high-pitched men counting blood currency and foreign weapons arsenals up for renewal. Before I could say, Be gone Gaggers, a large chandelier fell at my feet and the new Apple Watch I just bought on eBay got popped by a sniper hiding behind a rainfall of heavy burgundy drapes.

Damn, Gaggers, I shouted. The price for admission is the motherfucking price you'll have to pay, so I relieved myself on their fancy Sotheby's rug.

The war-mouthed Gaggers laughed and whistled from the ceiling where they clung like bats. I heard their repulsive toenails scratching all those gaudy fucking ceiling fixtures above me. They ate cantaloupe and stroked their dicks upside down. Drippings fell on my head, and in an instant, I found myself tumbling from a 68th-floor window.

Gaggers, I quickly learned, possess the uncanny ability to draw a precise chalk line of the human body milliseconds before they kill your ass. Preemptive cartography! Erasable public art! An outline of my gasping stature somehow sketched by the time my body sacked the pavement. I was so much smaller than I'd ever imagined myself to be: the sound of my body's impact was a nervous man's gulp. Snug as a condom the chalk line held my body. Between the womb and the tomb, I wish I could've had more sex, maybe even a child or two. And this was what saddened me, as I sat like a small heap of costume jewelry splattered across the avenue's sinister imagination.

Play

THE WOODEN BASEBALL BAT: I gave up a forest to live perpetually on the verge of living.

A FLUTTERING BAT TRAPPED AMONG THE STADIUM RAFTERS: I can't see your predicament, but I'll take your word for it. The hurt in your voice can't get me out of here fast enough. Now point me toward the open sky!

THE WOODEN BASEBALL BAT: Toward the open sky, you say? I see none; therefore, there is none.

[There is a Youtube Video]

There is a YouTube video of a tiny man sitting on the branch of a tiny silk oak tree on a tiny island near the equator.

And if you look closely enough, you'll notice that the tiny man's eyes are purple, and they are slightly crossed, because he is intoxicated by a river that flows from a childhood composed of an alcohol that quenches him like a tiny network of sloppy helixes threaded by ecstasy or pain depending on whom you ask and when.

On this tiny island there are tiny human beings clasping their hands to the steady recitation of prayer.

And on this tiny island there are tiny human beings wagging their fingers and blaming the tiny river for the atrocities of a tiny world.

If I could unseed the vast fields that mount the tiny flowers you gave me once to start this tiny novel all over again, I would.

I would.

TWO

The dream is the truth.
—Zora Neale Hurston

Los Kioskos

Three kiosks sit at the foot of a large, empty stadium parking lot. Three parking attendants converse while they wait. In the distance, a small outline of the stadium is visible. Cars never arrive. As a matter of fact, the parking attendants have been working days, weeks, months maybe, without attending to a single eventgoer.

The attendants cannot be seen in the kiosks because the windows are tinted. Each time they speak, the attendants slide open a plexiglass circle that allows the others, including the audience, to hear them.

Characters:
    Kiosk A
    Kiosk B
    Kiosk C

B:

Is this kiosk really a coffin, A?
Is it?

Just say it. If you think

it's a coffin,

I mean—

C: (Interjects) Just sleep tonight, B. We'll wake you if they come.

Scene 1

Early morning. The sun is bright. Clear day.

A: In my kiosk I've born a Rück's blue flycatcher.

C: I've got the Sumatran orangutan.

B: …I have a blue-fronted lorikeet.

A: …I, a Sumatran rhinoceros…

B: I have a Yangtze River Dolphin that paints silver portraits of its lips on my cash register.

C: I love the Western Lowland Gorilla! Her name's Lolly Madly, and she sings lullabies to the passing water beneath our feet.

B: A Vaquita!

A: A Hawksbill Sea Turtle!

B: Let's pack them in, my friends! Let's save the day!

A: Like a pagan's ark reveling in the sea!

B: (Protectively) Easy now. Now easy.

C: Let's do something, yes?

B: What's that, C?

A: (Excitedly) Go on and say it, C! Piledrive your words into our chests! Work that mighty intent up your throat and blast!

C: Let's do something now!

A: Say it!

C: Amigxs, I know we can certainly do it...

A and B: Say it!

A: Hurry, my tripas are curdling from the suspense.

B and C: Gross!

C: Let's close our eyes and think of the impossibilities of it. The possibility of the impossibility of really seeing it.

A: What do you mean, C? You've lost me. I give up. I'm about to faint. I've fainted. (Moans)

C: (Feigns frustration) Be patient. What I mean is, what will ultimately happen to the three of us?

A: Please explain—

C: (Goadingly) Please explain, A, says. Ok, please explain, A, says, I'll explain. This is just to say what will happen to the three valiant parking attendants who boldly dreamed of horses sowing plains?

A: Come again?

C: The muscular magic of automobiles begging entry? The piston push? The gas pedal pomp? The wild-hearted parking attendants whose sole mission was to rescue the general populace from toenail clippers and bad-smelling deodorant?

A: And don't forget the canned laughter!

C: I mean, like unicorns… and mermaids, maybe… like a wild stampede of Tonka trucks crawling over the many chins of mediocrity we'll be.

A: We wait.

B: And then?

A: We simply wait. This busy aviary will outgrow this kiosk in time. I can see it happening as it happens to mine. Planks are splitting. This rooftop is nearly an overheated radiator cap. The seams can no longer contain what they were meant to contain. Should I continue to wait? Should we continue to contain?

B: We feed them.

A: Feed them what?

B: Magic mushrooms. Chapulines. Imperial worms. Let's retrofit the terraces of our imaginations for our progeny to gaze from.

C: This event must happen soon. Do you think they'll come?

B: (Nervously) I can't see one vehicle approaching.

A: I do remember the days.

C: (Excitedly) How intense their arrival. I thought I'd break a limb. So many personalities. So many colorful jerseys, painted faces. The faded concert tees! The smiles! The anticipation! At least for one day no one cared about what they left behind. Say it loudly with me, at least for one day!

A, B, and C in unison: At least for one day!

B: But where are they now?

A: They're coming!

B: How do you know?

A: Why else would we be here?

B: Not sure.

A: Why would they pay us?

C: Do they?

A: We're here to serve the event. If there were no events planned to serve, what be our purpose?

B: Out of habit maybe?

A: (Incredulously) Out of habit?

B: Well you asked: "Why else would we be here?" And I simply asked out of habit maybe?

C: Does money have the capacity to create habits?

(They laugh.)

A: These menageries we've built are extraordinary, wouldn't you say? Imagine what we could charge to view them? I must admit though—

B: (Quizzingly) Admit though what?

A: I'm nearly out of room.

B: Maybe that's the event we should all hope for.

C: (Sudden shift in tone) Don't invite such a spectacle. Imagine what they would do to such a thing. They ruin everything. They trample and stumble and grovel without ever considering a single consequence. Everything is expendable these days. Objects of momentary desire. Like children these heads that drive.

A: Hyperbole!

B: Expendable like us?

A: Speak for yourself. I'm a unique attribute.

B: We all are. There are none of us more valuable.

A: Are you rubbing your chin, C? C, have you chewed your fingernails?

C: You do know something of me, don't you?

A and B together: We do.

C: Easily distracted is what I'm saying.

A and B together: We do!

C: Not me. Them! Where are they now? Probably marinating at some venue near a strange coast, considering the new show in town. I bet near an RV park with closed-circuit television and blue-haired phonies taking tickets at a rubber door that smells of engine oil.

B: Perhaps a Hunger Artist…

(They laugh.)

C: Or an old man with angel's wings…

(They laugh louder.)

A: They search for windmills!

(They laugh.)

B: I think we're too hard on them.

C: Perhaps. But they do deserve some level of reproach. I'm thinking the tyrants.

A: The tyrants, eh? The tyrants are within all of us really.

C: Vladimir!

B: Estragon!

A: Pozzo!

B: Yuck! That old scold!

C: Luck!

(All): Godot! (They laugh.) (All). To dog a dog is simply repeating itself!
(They laugh.)

B: Which of us is leashed?

C: You are! Leashed to your bloated and babbling scripture du jour.

A: Oh, come on, C. Be light.

C: (Arrogantly) I be light in books, I say. Dynamite beneath the reading
lamp! I am the gunpowder bowels of truth!

A: When do they come? (Suddenly worried.) By the time they arrive, we
might be demented. We might be slobbering fools!

C: I think you've arrived.

A: I'm writing my living will as we speak. B and C, I leave to you this kiosk
and all of its appendages.

(They laugh.)

C: My leash is glittered.

A: My leash encircles the great Gulf and brings its breezes to me.

Scene 2

Schubert's "Ave Maria" plays softly until it descends to inaudibility.

B: Can you believe I used to wear gloves? Remember the amount of money we exchanged? The number of tickets we sold?

C: Reminisce!

A: The amount of times I counted my drawer—constantly afraid that my cash register would someday come up short. I spent hours after everyone left, recounting, recounting, recounting...

C: And now we recount, those were the days.

A: ...recounting, recounting, recounting...

B: Memory is like a fountain. Though how long shall it runneth?

C: My friend's mother lost her memory long before she died. I admired her for years. I once promised I'd write her biography. Incredible woman. A photojournalist. She published her work in some of the most reputable magazines on the planet.

A: Hyperbole!

B: No...please continue.

C: She captured the lives of Dionte County. The poverty. The people's resilience. The environmental racism. If not for her, policies would have never been drafted. A bold and beautiful clarion. We need her still. Without her, we shrink that much more.

A: Thousand Times Broken.

C: Exactly.

B: Did you ever begin her biography?

C: Nothing beyond a few brief sketches. Now there's no way to retrieve that information. I was too late.

B: It's never too late.

C: I suppose so. I suppose I owe it to her. (Reassuringly though distant; reciting).

> It's too late : : it's never too late
> It's too late : : it's never too late
> It's too late : : it's never too late
>
> It's too late

Scene 3

Silence. The Kiosk attendants are napping, though they never admit it. Over time, an unspoken arrangement was agreed upon that whenever there was silence, there was silence between them. Rarely there is silence, however, because all of them talk in their sleep.

Scene 4

A: Last night I discovered three licks to a wombat's belly can transform a Lego metropolis into a heated mining operation on the slope of a hill. Such strange alchemy. Did I ever tell you my family was a bundle of miners in a small town? Copper. Turn of the century Mexico. They worked beneath the earth and now they sleep there eternally. My kiosk reroutes air to the tunnels that link my family to god. There, I've said it.

B: You did. I heard it. Your first mention. Does your kiosk account for climate change?

A: I'm not a scientist, but I can assess the damage of your barbs, B. In this atmosphere we create honey.

C: I've leveraged a balloon factory in my kiosk. A committed and brilliant labor movement has changed things here for the better. Production and morale are up. More importantly, each worker is paid more than the CEO I keep cuffed and gagged in the broom closet. Balloons will soon float above us like a thousand thought bubbles. No event will go un-surveilled, I mean, thought of.

(They laugh. They groan. They quiet for one whole minute, sadness overcomes them.)

B: (Refocused and excitedly) That is great. Tell me how it feels to be among such dedicated creatives.

C: Model. That's all you need. Just like us, unwavering, stalwart.

A and B: Ah—

C: And a river of mezcal! (Offering shots of mezcal to laborers.). Here you go. Here's one for you. And you. And you. Easy now, you've got to take it easy… but drink up. To prosperity! Memory is a fountain that runs over the lip of my shot glass. ¡Arriba, abajo, al centro, pa'dentro!

A: That's awful!

C: I'm kidding. We only drink the word. As long as it is impeccable.

A: I have a pair of binoculars lodged in my mind. Someone built them. What's ahead is bleak. I'll look backwards. But better now to look forward. I look forward to look backward. Though better now to look nowhere.

B and C: But here!

C: Can you see automobiles? Can you see chartered busses? Circus tents? Can you see a fleet of sailboats cutting distance away like a cancerous ear?

B: What about dogma? Can you make out a resurrection?

A: It's hazy, but the boots are leather heavy.

C: Could it be a metal concert in the making?

A: Hooves lumber beside them. Scampering jack rabbit paws I make out though barely.

C: Who are the promoters?

B: (Convinced) It might be a test. It must be a test.

A: (Fearful) My goodness, the air is thick, grey powder. I've seen such things in my basement. When my contractor's liver failed, every word he spoke hinged on soot and angry memory. Cellular memory I'm convinced and say to you now.

B and C: Hyperbole!

B: Think of the event that is on its way.

Scene 5

C: Wait! I see something.

B: Where?

C: Out there!

A: What is it?

C: My mother, I believe. She's looking for me.

A: Didn't you tell her you're working?

C: I did. I've written her though the postal service has not arrived in—

A: (Excited) Please describe her. What is she wearing? You're not going to leave us, are you?

C: —in some time, I suppose. A blue dress. Paint is splattered across the lower half. A painter she is. Did I ever tell you my mother knew Georgia O'Keefe?

A and B: No.

C: Miguel Covarrubias?

A and B: No.

C: Lola Álvarez Bravo?

B: Who are they?

A: Yes, who are they? Are they performers?

C: They are great artists. My mother included. Her figurative works are miraculous.

A: Hyperbole.

C: I know, I know. But there she is.

B: I don't see anything.

A: Neither do I.

C: Seeing has never been part of our duty.

B: That's what I say most of the time.

A: Please don't offer B ammunition. B might float away and entangle himself in a blurry nest of angels' pubic hair.

C: A rivalry, my mother had. Did I ever tell you my mother was a mathematician? The letters she wrote filled me with continuous equations. Don't ask me what they meant, but beauty on the page.

A: What was the rivalry about?

C: Who saw was the rivalry.

B: Who saw?

A: Then seeing. There's the rivalry. There lies the drama between artists.

B: I feel certain in my inner sight.

A: We know you do, B. Your inner sight is an equation unto itself.

C: The irregular heartbeat is yours, B. That's why we love you.

B: Thanks C. That means a lot coming from you.

A: (Critically) But you told us that your mother is an artist.

B: You did, C. Please keep your stories straight.

C: Exactly. I did tell you she's an artist. And that is what the rivalry is about.

A: I'm not following. Are you following, B?

B: I'm following a topsy-turvy path.

A: (Grunts)

C: My mother is an artist *and* a mathematician. She's a glorious doubling.

A: Hyperbole!

C: My mother's rivalry is with herself if you could believe it. When she faces a mirror…like an old-fashioned gunfight, she draws quickly, and then she is dead.

B: Ahh.

A: An eccentric. That explains a lot.

C: Come again.

A: Well, that explains a lot about you.

C: Me?

A: Yes, all that preoccupies you. Is your mother arriving today?

C: I haven't seen my mother in eighteen years.

B: That explains a lot.

C: Come again.

B: Yes, all that preoccupies you. Is your mother arriving today?

C: My mother is on the road. She conducts a symphony and she is touring the Galápagos—

A and B guffaw in disbelief.

Scene 6

C: What are you doing, B? I hear a drill.

B: I'm building a surface-to-air missile defense system.

A: Why?

B: In case we're attacked from the sky. Vehicles are not arriving, A. They must feel unsafe. They must fear.

A: Who would ever want a missile defense system at an event?

B: That's the question they—.

A: (Interjects) And the they you're thinking of?

B: I'm also building a monsoon season to wash away the fears.

C: (Excitedly) There you go. You're on it now. I'll build a shipwreck and invite all of the cruelest to visit and then leave them there. We don't need them here. A shipwreck where prehistoric crocodiles play chess. Where gawking snorkelers swim too close to the reptilian tension until their arms are bitten off…Pow!… Bare backs crushed like ice cubes…Crack! Stack 'em up, those gawking snorkelers, those petty snorkelers.

A: Ok…Then I'll build a 19th-century sanatorium to house all of the death merchants. Where's my hammer? I drew up the blueprints days ago, and now I can't find them. Where's my organist? I pay an organist to play for me whenever I conceive a new idea. Organist! Where are you organist? Come out now before it's too late.

The organist plays "Ave Maria."

B: I hope the event doesn't start soon, because we sure do have a lot of work to do.

A: I'm drawing folks. I never told you this before. I was great friends with Georgia O'Keefe, Miguel Covarrubias and Lola Álvarez Bravo.

(They laugh.)

My hand is loose and fine. My cursive is to die for. I'm writing a letter to B's god. Dear B's god, we are here now and waiting for the sign we'll build for you. Sunny days are ahead, and our tiny monuments are erected to serve even in their darkest ways. Dear B's god, let's host an event and invite all of the world's cows. We'll even dress up like cows and join them in the middle of the stadium. A cow MC. A cow governing board. A cow that sings the universal cow anthem, followed by a cow manifesto. Cows that sneak up behind the stage and surprise the crowd of cows who wait at the edges of their sleep.

C: Dear B's god, we'll call it a festival of cows. We'll shut down the factory farms for one day. Allow the cows to exist freely, so far from cruelty. We'll lose the hamburgers and spit out the milk. I've invited a delegation of proud cows from the district of cow to preside over the crafting of the constitution of cows. Who will be there, A?

A: A cow ventriloquist.

B: A cow orthodontist.

A: A cow psychologist.

B: A cow mystic.

A: A revolutionary cow.

B: A cow saint.

A: A bus load of sanitary worker cows because we're not cleaning up after a bunch of cows.

B: A holy cow!

C: A cow surgeon.

A: A cow scientist who invents shampoo for cows that makes cow meat repulsive to the bite.

B: This event will be an a-cow-pocolypse. Cows will be non-consumptive forever!

C: Our event is a winner. Let's draw up the plans and sing a hundred songs for the fantasy.

(The organist plays.)

B: My kiosk is harboring rain clouds but I have no doubt these days are
   derived from light.

Scene 7

B: (Worried) What if they don't show up?

A: They will.

B: What if they don't?

A: If we've built it they'll come.

C: We are no bodies. We're nothing but boxes with arms and hands extended from them. Who are we to will an extraordinary event?

A: But we have.

C: We have not.

A: We have. None of this will be forgotten.

B: As long as we live, and from what we leave behind, is encountered like a seashell on a sea of black beach sand.

A: Amen.

C: I see.

B: I told you so.

Scene 8

C:
I'm driving a green tank
through your toy piano store, A.
Better think
before it comes

Hot hay bale quick
this yellow giant just
spit from its mouth.

B: What's coming?

C: It's not what you think, B.

A: I had no choice about it.

B: About what?

C: The honeycomb in A's throat, his mother. The honeycomb A keeps there
   called home.

B: A mother?

A: When will the herds arrive?

C: You stutter, and I think of your honeycomb. Where does it go? How inseparable they've become. That insecurity that never dies.

A: My mother was forced to write "I will not speak Spanish in school" three hundred times on a green chalkboard.

B: Hyperbole!

C: At school, my great-grandfather hid under the middle school bleachers to eat the burritos his mother packed him for lunch each day. Alone, he was teased and—

B: Hyperbole!

A: Your tombstone will read what, B?

B: (Silence)

Scene 9

B: Tonight, I'm cartwheeling beneath the moon. Can you see me?

C: Like a harp, I strum the elegance of an intimate era closeted in your arms. Swing with me tonight, B. Let's jam the airwaves with our sighs.

A: You two have some nerve commanding space with that sloppy sap.

B: Please stop, A, so we can percuss the consonants of your name with our bodies' bends and folds.

A: My kiosk is raining tonight.

C: As is mine. The watch tower I built is bearing the weight.

A: Of sight and light.

C: Yes.

B: Love stains just like our teeth though we still chew. Do you, A?

A: I'm alone and it's raining in my kiosk. I'm wet all over. Buffalo hide in the basement with their artists. Over the hill my mother winks from the asparagus fields and will never see our event. Tonight, I'm going to build a catapult and sling piles of cotton wool at the violence of their hearts.

C: Who's there?

A: They're there, find some time to unwind the mind—they're there, they're there.

Scene 10

C: This kiosk is just another funeral parlor.

A: Don't say that.

B: Let's close our eyes and—

C: (Angered.) Don't you dare, B. I'm sending a subway to collect my love.

B: But why?

C: Because you're unflattering.

B: Please don't betray the helix, C. My kiosk will crack. My four-chambered love is the architect of a neutron bomb.

A: Hyperbole!

C: When it arrives, leave the flowers there. And I want the miner's lamp and the cabin near the sea.

B: Silence will be your welcome.

C: So be it. So then silence be my goodbye.

Scene 11

A answers questions in his Kiosk. The sound of a box fan can be heard.

What's that?
That's a school.
What's that?
That's a honeysuckle.
What's that?
That's a fire department.
What's that?
That's a mountain.
What's that?
That's a fire escape.
What's that?
That's a tiger drinking water from the palm of a child.
What's that?
That's a volcano shouting can you hear me to the astronaut eternally
    tethered to Mars.
What's that?
That's a dime-sized dimple.
What's that?
That's a little doggie making us all feel better.
What's that?
That's a little house with chimney smoke.
What's that?
That's a gallon of soy milk forgotten on the hood of a car.

What's that?

That's a costume for a play about healing.

What's that?

That's a giant river collecting names and places along its windy journey.

What's that?

Those are the names and places we've been.

Are you a river?

Come again.

Are you a river?

I'm not a river.

What's that?

That's a rainstorm like a little wig that sits on a sad zebra's head.

Are you a rainstorm?

Come again.

Are you a rainstorm?

I'm a rainstorm.

What kind of rainstorm are you?

I'm the rainstorm that fills the river.

Scene 12

B: I woke up this morning and couldn't find my legs.

A: Asleep again?

B: My legs, not I.

C: Were they hacked off again by the gang of supercharged dildos in your sleep?

A: I hear the vibrations of their crime in the walls.

(They laugh.)

B: I'm miserable.

A and C: Hyperbole!

B: But my legs are here beneath my waist though not so much love to use them.

A: Dip them in a pool. You've dug up a pool in your kiosk, haven't you?
   You've bragged before. I've heard the water swell. Like a couple of teabags,
   let them in and let them begin.

B: My spooky legs have returned: ungrateful limbs! They've trampled all over
   my handmade paper. (On the verge of crying.) I broke my back all night
   working on this Pondicherry paper and now—

A and C: Hyperbole!

A: What was the paper for?

B: (Lucidly) For the drawings I made.

C: Drawings?

B: I drew a Ferris wheel last night. A had a basket. C had a basket. I had a basket. Each of us had a Ferris wheel basket. Our colorful baskets shaped like ears to listen to the world from. Other baskets were occupied by a team of musical instruments. Birds landed on our shoulders. Butterflies lived in a contrabass. A, you sang a song about a river in Managua. C, you blew kisses at the moon that stuck to its surface. And if you could imagine it, those on Earth suddenly had a twittering butterfly collection to look at as they waited for a bumbling recital of keys. Then my legs stepped on them: the paper; the carousel; the butterfly-pecked moon; my great grandfather's x-ray of lungs blackened by pesticide.

A and C: Hyperbole!

B: I see. Did I mention my legs are former lovers?

A: Let's call them Hamlet and Ophelia.

C: No, I vote Hansel and Gretel! They must be Hansel and Gretel!

B: These stickers on my legs. Where did they come from?

C: I shipped them around the world, and then they wrote back as you
   slept tirelessly on the dire lawn of (slowly and exaggeratedly)
   MEL-AN-CHO-LY.

B: (Sighs)

Scene 13

C: (Loud and inspired)
First, I'll draw the right coronary artery near the atrium
And then I'll draw the right ventricle nice and easy—
And then I'll sketch a White House with little suited men
standing on its rooftop hoarding boredom in their pockets
And then I'll draw a pulmonary trunk, and like a sad sac,
I'll invite a locomotive to pull our troubles away
Up comes the ascending aorta, the love sax,
Inferior vena cava like PVC pipe I'll construct running through the woods
Envision a broken window on top with little hair that sprouts near the mitral
Hallelujah sings the pulmonary artery inching toward the double-breasted
     suit in a pine bed
And I'll map the ventricular septum with a Sharpie, a dozen bullets,
and a can of thumbtacks
that read like Braille's love letters along the alleyways of the pericardium
I'll add stewards at the bypass who prepare endearing utterances stitched
by their flawless handiwork
To the rhythm of the assembly center, conveyor belt
To the chorus line of cog and corpuscle
The chimney sweeper who tidies the apex before Victory's Liquor
shutters as we always knew it would
And Oh hi, they'll say, and Oh hi, we'll say,
on this penultimate oven-baked morning
In these streets wild inside the music box in all of us,
where a factory sings and then shuts

Scene 14

C: In my kiosk I've drawn an Addax.

A: I have an Alabama cavefish.

B: The rhinoblue-throated macaw!

C: The Brazilian merganser brown spider monkey reporting for duty!

B: My Imperial woodpecker has taken to poker... It's a delight to hear the Cherrywood table tap incessantly like a wild Morse code signaling victory.

A: I have an ivory-billed woodpecker that shares its spirit with an activist on the frontlines of doubt.

C: Listen to my Philippine crocodile chatter its teeth. When it hears the windchimes I hung from my mother's harp strings, it chat-chats-chat-chat-chat-chats... chat-chats-chat-chat-chat-chats.

A: My southern bluefin tuna is a sleepwalker.

C: Drumroll please. Allow me to introduce you to the saiga antelope angel...

A and B: Hello saiga antelope angel. We love you!

C: Ah, he's crying. We're all crying. The dams have broken.

A: Let's all cry. Let's wash ourselves with what we have in ourselves.

C: Let it out saiga antelope angel. Let's float our boats with tears.

B: The lake is rising. My Mediterranean monk seal is laughing through her Pondicherry lágrimas.

A: This life is ours to protect.

B and C: This life is ours to protect. Bam!

C: I see my mother, and she's sleeping with Georgia O'Keefe.

B: And Miguel Covarrubias?

A: Such flowers!

B: And Lola Álvarez Bravo?

A: Such wondrous flowers.

C: Our mothers of the flowers contained in our constructions.

A: Goodnight you two.

B: Goodnight you two.

C: Goodnight you two. This event was finally shared.

A: This event happened one day and then was gone.

A, B, and C: Poof!

The end.

THREE

Poem Unanimous

Perhaps it's hiding beneath a bed somewhere in Montevideo
Or maybe it fled deep into a dark tunnel's clandestine suck,
equipped with closed-circuit television, central heating and air
Who knows where it went is what I'm saying,
standing guard at Buckingham Palace: tall, black,
furry hat, you know the kind, mummed up
for tourists, imperialism personified, straight as a Ticonderoga pencil
Or maybe it's riding a Vespa against oncoming traffic up Holly-
wood Blvd, nursing a slight bender, saggy paunch and red-faced—
If you hear from that damn navy-blue sock gone missing from my drawer,
tell it I've moved on, bought
an '81 Chrysler, went to the movies,
built a rocket ship out of Nestor's hydro supplies
and three gallons of glue; tell it I've opened
a tortaría on Mt. Everest's summit point where we've
assembled a metropolis of beefy mariachis to usher in
the resurrection of large-scale resistance in the key of C,
tell it I ate a map of the United States,
rolled it up, digested its entire settler colonial history in one swallow
then excreted the whole shebang
in a single whiff, outer space,
into the fifth dimension, to enable
us to move on and begin again
though never, ever permitted
to forget

Who knows where it went,
they'll say, but of the darkness,
some great light will ready its wings
and stretch wide in the very absence
of the thing

New beginnings where all feet resemble warm, tender clocks

New beginnings where all feet are loved beyond the grizzly foundation
that once promised to engulf them.

Bird Brain

Amá, Amá, I'm a lemon. Each morning I hear my footsteps
leave the house hot on their escape route, my spirit,
dysentery in blue jeans. Un par
de pinche acid wash.

Amá, Amá, I can't fuck.
I can't fuck.
Apá, Apá, I can't love.

These chocolate fangs couldn't short a string of Christmas lights
with their mushy bite.

Nobody will give me the time. I'm a gym hat absent of throttle.
A blood brigade ekes out my ears.

Life's graceless gossiping mocks my wet sock.
Look at that full moon growling at us, gargantuan white rabbit,
severe door knob disabling my Francis Ponge door.
This piccolo couldn't play one bar of good sex music.
My mid-center is a shuttered car lot.
My balloon-release, an uneventful nanosecond!
Faint explosions hiccup over the sea. I've never had a speeding ticket.
My brain is a nervous dick deterrent. I'll never satisfy. O sigh,
O sigh, in the clearing, I'm on one knee and screaming:
Devour me grass flowers and hand grenades, yardstick birth,
devour me bloodthirsty infantry

over the bluff, devour me,
psycho nails, gravedigger shovel, devour me,
blood pile of bird-brain feathers, juicy phantasma.

My wet frown is a hot curling iron sipping bathwater.
Sycophants live in my ears. They don't pay rent, hack my inner jukebox,
and play nowhere music in nowhere time out of time.
Somehow, I've created a discotheque of wooden ships that splinter the darkness
with their arrhythmic fight songs. Unfathomable disaster, my napkin
smells like polyester, devour me, lonely cock, eat right
and exercise near the sick lamp, don't be afraid of my hula hoop,
friend of the coco powder sage collapsed of stage fright just before the soliloquy.

Oh, that Ghost just stole my tuna fish! Every day an ounce of gold   (god)
is left on my doorstep. The grab is the trick.
Poof, and a cathedral of lint! Who controls the bell toll?
Who feeds the rats? Who waters the mangy tire iron?
Who pits the salami against the vegetarian?
Who dances for love? Who chases the lactose
from my cousin Nestor's dingy fridge?
Who blames the manic teachers, the lousy equations, the near-sighted engineers
of thick rigor mortis lab coats on math class ceilings?
Who sings blood hues of the blues? Who leapt
from the diving board to realize it was only glass?

Have you heard about the high-flying parkour angels in overalls and chanclitas
who love to write fables in my checking account?

Seriously, my debt is a .38 pointed at my sex organ.

Follow me, I might be dying. The fuck
is a hairy hood ornament doing on my Monte Carlo?

Last night I fell from the same second story window; in a frenzy,
I smoked hash. Grew my hair back, and
ate my wallet, all before impact. Empty car lot. Bankrupt airline.
Arcade meth attendant: there are no quarters in this machine.

Of all the rain falling on this planet I've somehow attracted
the neon spacey kind that governs like a syllabus of smoke.

Green Water

I. Green Water

Nestor once told me that the most unique heroes in life are the ones filled with fragrant water.

Nestor said: And you know what, mijito, when they inevitably acquire their bullet holes, that greenish liquid that smells of hibiscus and revolution's camouflage will exit their bodies and nourish the soil your *punk ass* walks on. What grows from your footsteps is the question.

Mmmm, I droned. I couldn't think of any other way to respond. Nestor didn't expect me to either, he never expected me to. He was the talker, and I, the faithful listener, the documentarian, the archivist, the dutiful, leather-bound artifact awaiting discovery.

Nestor stared at the floor and grinned, still speaking, if you could believe, without ever moving his lips.

In time, for no reason I can explain, my hand raised toward the high desert sun that leaned softly into the palm of my hand. Like that, I thought of nothing but salt. And the wild taste of self-preservation.

II. The Landing

Nestor landed in a volcanic crater in El Salvador when he fell head first from the sky.

At once, birds mobilized and congregated in Ceiba trees. They strategized and drew elaborate plans to rescue him with a raft made of discarded tires and burlap bags stolen from nearby coffee plantations in Ataco.

News of the event reached Langley, Virginia, where an irreverent votive was promptly lit and placed on a desktop before an intelligence agency of unrelenting believers cloaked in omniscient data points and blood-wrecked axe handles could surround a man issuing orders through a thick huff of cigar smoke. Instructed to categorize and subdue the conspiring birds, agents impersonated good-willed ornithologists after hastily fabricating advanced degrees to update their emphysemic vitaes, the stench of chlorophyll already emanating from their hair.

In a single week, they planned for the elimination of all birds and the re-education of trees.

III. Nestor's Dream

Like a haze
of lucíernagas fall-
ing, thousands
of us,
slipping in-
to a green ocean's
tight-lipped
horizon

Flickering, Nestor said,
is how we'll ultimately
go down

       Flickering,

and again,
flickering

when we return
again

IV. The Sketch

Nestor sketched a clandestine aviary on his clipboard: remarkable architecture, thriving vegetation, colorful dwellings for an immense chamber of winged inhabitants.

Then, with a sigh, Nestor planned for the spontaneous sublimation in the event of the probable siege.

V. They Found Something

They found a crooked spoke that belonged to Nestor's beloved bicycle in a landfill two miles out of town when a swarm of ants loosened the abduction's mystery like a persistent wrecking ball.

They found his umbrella at a rural bus station after a thousand bullets fell from the sky and quenched a death squad's interminable lust for iron.

They found his comb that smelled of ginger and that grew antennas during lettuce season on a space station platform near the moon.

They found his retainer on a cliff near a waterfall: remnants of quartz, and the ignorant DNA of a rabid breed of wealthy safari hunters.

And they discovered his wings in a storage unit on Hollywood Blvd. Eagle-like, patinaed appendages that shook themselves awake when LAPD SWAT kicked open the door and quickly surrounded them: "Hands up!" they demanded. Wherein the wings replied: "We're Goya's oeuvre, and we will not be apprehended today," before escaping through the gap in the fat captain's teeth.

Poem

1

The sky spelled out my name in scratches, and now Nestor's pissed at me. Nestor's teeth fell out. I said, Nestor, your teeth fell out, and now Nestor's pissed at me. We fell into an outrageously long silence until I pointed, reminding Nestor, Hey, Nestor, look at the sky, the sky spelled out my name in colorful scratches, and now Nestor's pissed at me. Nestor said, Looks like some tempestuous child left a handful of Crayolas to melt on the hood of a Jaguar. A Jaguar, eh, why a Jaguar? *Pffft*. A Jaguar was the first make that came to mind, and now Nestor's pissed at me.

2

Nestor said, If you must know, my teeth have been falling out for years. Say what, and now Nestor's pissed at me. My teeth began to loosen when I was in the womb, falling like rain. When I least expected it, they fell, they fell like rain. Have you ever felt your teeth fall like rain? Have you ever felt your mouth rain? In my dreams, I suppose, and now Nestor's pissed at me. Sometimes they shatter like old wine jugs across the sidewalk of my childhood stomp and gag whenever I stumble back from the liquor store, he laughed. I laughed, too, and now Nestor's pissed at me.

3

I said, The sky is white, this blue is so light, and what is that green square humming in the corner near the faded moon, and now Nestor's pissed at me.

4

Nestor is a spectacular ventriloquist!
Sometimes he makes my mind speak!
Sometimes he becomes a church and a whole singing congregation!
Sometimes he makes the great big oak converse with the telephone wire near
the liquor store!
Sometimes he makes the clouds chat!

5

Nestor's got that big ear, that precise ear, that quetzal ear, that bandleader ear,
that mellifluous vox trap, that mellified honey maker, that oracle orifice, that
audio dynamite—

6

Once Nestor transformed a patch of sky into the green room of a mythical
comedy club in heaven. Everyone there: Pryor, Carlin, Cantínflas, Bruce, Red
Fox, and... But wait, what about the women, I asked, and now Nestor's…

O egregious omission, but Nestor apologized, not to me exactly, but at the
edge of the cliff, to someone or something out there, and then he returned,
and had me laughing—thereafter that is—until his mouth rained, and once
again, we were left to stand on a thin horizon without umbrellas where teeth
chipped our shoulder blades, and a strange diminishing man stood to our
side and sang of lost loves and failed aeration and gone booze.

7

Then the clouds began to die, and the scratches and the itches and the melted Crayolas on the hood of a Jaguar left by some tempestuous child seemed like an ordinary thing strewn across an ordinary sky, which meant it was time to return to work, and to hear the punch of timecards again, and to clack back to the sound of digitalization, which really meant, belts, cogs, factory whistles, and smokestacks called by another name; while all the while, Nestor's teeth continued to plink, plink, plank along the Pacific coastline, like a magnificent holiday of sound, like an ice truck filling up an ocean with its hulky pelagic grammar for all of us to drink from.

The Insurmountable

The world might be motherfucking cuckoo but my homeboy Nestor's not that's for sure.

Nestor's just the neighborhood peludo inching in the dark like some mole in time.

My boy Nestor's smart as fuck and his science might very well explain why there's a jungle in my kitchen where a three-headed monster shakes ass deep bamboo trees behind my refrigerator just to frighten me.

This morning an insincere warthog stole a jar of Nutella from my snack drawer and thought it funny to leave a note that read: "Your rent's due motherfucker."

I saw a wolverine nursing a fox last week while I reached for a glass of almond milk so beautifully tender in the twilight until a slick-mouthed lemur mimicked my end-of-the-month complaints about the rising water bill with pinche helium in its mouth.

This kitchen is a shit-talking ostrich provoking the goofy-eyed vulture perched high up to double down and dine on my life insurance policy.

This kitchen is a blue-haired stoner smoking herb with a marsupial intent on pocketing all of my cutlery.

I spend most mornings spraying mosquito repellant all over my trembling body before an hour wasted clearing ocotillo bushes with a machete just to deliver my beloved panecito to the toaster.

Damn those scandalous-ass hyenas with those beach-ball laughs!

What kind of forest is this, Nestor?

Nestor says I have no imagination and that I'd die before I had even lived if I'm not careful with what I have. Whatever the fuck that means.

If only Nestor could devise a rocket ship with all that science he thinks I'd buy admission tickets for me and the me's I might leave behind to lift off my kitchen countertop and soar some place I've never truly been, divorced of the down-here-dull-on-gravity-me, O hey to kick and paw wildly at the sun.

Overcoming a forest in my kitchen is insurmountable. Nestor taught me that word. *I believe it isn't as insurmountable as previously thought to actually inhabit the moon,* he said, *but I would never-ever do that you know why?* Why Nestor, why? I asked. *It's because my father already sees enough of that astronomical darkness in me,* and I liked that, all sciency and shit, but Chicano goth at the same time, con ese corazonsote Nestor possesses beneath his pecho like a little-little ashtray that tries hard-hard-hard to pacify a night of burning cities in its grasp.

But for real, Nestor needs to break up with books from time to time. Break up with those motherfuckers, I say. Too many in your head and they become battery acid for the brain. I swear I hear pages flipping inside his dome while he's standing on the front porch saying nothing, perhaps, daydreaming about the great oceanic enervations of the intergalactic psyche, perhaps, as he likes to say while using his favorite word, perhaps. Of course, I can only assume, perhaps, but one thing's for sure, he's always still, javelin-straight, an obelisk on the street corner of eternity, and I doubt he'll ever put down those damn books not even for one hot-ass minute. But that joint I borrowed about growing mushroom gardens in kitchen cabinets *wow* and now my visions have declared sovereignty.

O Nestor's bear traps around my broiler to protect the steaks he's been manning but I'm vegetarian! That meat's for the dying lion, he says, though I've never seen it nor do I ever want to. The thought of an accidental encounter makes me shiver. We must always think about the dying lion in the light, he said, and when I look at Nestor's eyes as he reports this shit I can tell he means it. And this is what hurts me for reasons I cannot openly express in a poem written from the jungle of my days.

Nestor visits me most late afternoons just to set meat on the kitchen floor for a lion that might never roar anymore. This nonsense Nestor's grown in my kitchen fills me with great anguish though I must admit the air I breathe these days embodies glorious pine needle, glorious honey, glorious and wild lavender that just startles me into living. I exist to revere this plight—Nestor's dream, nightmare meat for the willing.

The Looks

There are Looks in the fences. They stink of menace and iron work.

I remember when the Looks called me names like: Glue   Cross Bones   Fly Trap

Days I walked home from school dreaming of levity and impenetrable door jambs.

But the Looks are conniving baseball bats they swing for the head.

In high school everything was a drug that looked at me:

My teachers did drugs. Our Parent Association did drugs. I couldn't inherit the
Monday-Friday logic.

I wanted to tear it out my throat and challenge that pathological logos: *Criticize
me to my face!*

Once I fell drunk on Nestor's shadow and felt it wince beneath my back.

Nestor said: There are few good people in the world.

Nestor said: *The only difference between a truth and a lie is that the lie hasn't
happened yet.*

Please disaffect me. I wouldn't mind a disappearing act if only to re-emerge on
the moon.

That Look enjoying me when it really should have said:

I'm an FBI looking in there

I'm a CIA looking in there

I'm a two-way polonium surveillance window looking in there

I'm a furious cop fink looking in there.

A nowhere goon tails me these days.

I hear it licking stolen SIM cards above me from a weather balloon:

That autoblaster. That suction mack. Everything is hazy. The Looks are real.

I used to be a mighty stockyard hero but now my forklift sleeps ungassed,

heeds the timesheet imaginary, heckles the reckless bottle.
The Looks are severe. The Looks are willy-nilly and intent
on lighting matches from my earlobes just to brighten their dopey-looking glass.

with a line borrowed from José Olivarez

FOUR

Poetry is another way of writing in sand.
—John Yau

The Bullets

Ernie the Painter carved a bullet from a small milk carton and saved it for
a rainy day when everything would become wet and disintegrate and drink
from the sky

O Denim bullet

O Woolen bullet

O Venetian-Velvet bullet

Sticky weather and polyurethane mitten bullet

Bullets of sand
of salad greens
of dimpled cheek

Bullets of blood cells rattling among the interior of the human harp

of heartbreak
of baby wipes
of hollow bone chime and mechanical pencil lead

Bullets of the imagination released like a silver waterfall from a sleeper's ear—

Bedtime harbor!

Infantry of bullets sewn of old sweaters and its pledge to keep us warm

Bullets that walk into the sawdust rink and align themselves according to height and depth,

until one clears its throat. And then they're off—pow!—a singing bunch,

lyrics about the world and the stars and the universe and the promise to reject the compositions of another violent kind of work

The Education

Ghost Teacher calls me Permanently Unfinished.

Ghost Rector nicknames me Tiny Incapable.

A fallen ghost basically adds up to nothing *1 1 1.*

Our eyelashes fall and our voices drip from the inner faucets of ourselves a
few times and then no more.

Sometimes I feel like an empty speech bubble. An invisible comic strip so
no one laughs.

Many of us simply want to read our poetry by the river *1 1 1.*

Many of us want to say so long to this curriculum without fingerprints nor
with one last breath spared.

Many of us just want to read our poetry by the river, to close our eyes and
be just as such.

after Kim Hyesoon

The Foot Parade

The Sentients ate my field of apricots and flowered the evening with their
 blue breath.

Their silence and inability to apologize is a poem dedicated to space travel
 and irreverent bunnies.

A little, yellow book sits by my desk lamp and listens to me agonize over this
 month's electric bill.

Hands wave from the other side of a glass door fogged with pulled pork breath.

Who are the Sentients? my pops asked. And why did they choose you?
 Look at them, the way they grasp that soil with their ashy hands and feed
 it to each other.

If the poem's origins are quiet enough, you'll see.

This is silence's soliloquy upended and thirsty for more. It widens beyond the
 palm frond tattooed on my neighbor's back like an antenna dispatching
 chisme to the moon.

Access love like a wading swan inventing grass.

You devoured a clock and a box of cigars while my inner city plowed through
 an angry sea mob of waves and cement boots.

Silver fish sleep in grass hustling trigger-ready harpists in their dreams.

You undid the green that made the grass a hero of us all when our only duty
was to maintain the grasses' greenness.

I heard the purple flower music again, then died, a scent they dragged out
the door.

FIVE

Two and a half weeks is all it took for Weecho's initials to return to the top: letters aglow, pushing through the depths of a black screen in ominous, buzzing, moth-ball white:

—W.M...Biaaatch!

Dispatches:
From the Hive of the Bee

1.

Weecho socked Iggy across the forehead when he finally caught up to him on 4th street aiming at a blue and white cloudy Iggy had had his eyes on all spring semester. Before this cataclysmic encounter, Iggy knelt quietly, a Zen master in ocean-deep meditation, with one eye closed, his lucky cat's eye boulder cocked in his thumb, ready to win another monumental game of "ringer." This was the canica game that we played in our neighborhood that instantaneously drew thick demarcations between legends and losers for generations to come. When what seemed to be like an inevitable victory, Weecho picked Iggy's bony ass up from the dirt lot we used exclusively for these types of marble games and after-school rumbles, and popped the top of Iggy's dome with a quick flurry of coscorrones that gave birth to a cartoonish, high-rise chichón. In one swift motion, Weecho snatched Iggy by the neck and guided him straight back to 7-Eleven while shaking him every so often to accent a colorful phrase he uttered. Iggy shuffled next to Weecho defenselessly, and the crowd left behind watched defenselessly, for they all knew Iggy would soon bear the weight that so many generations of the bullied and beaten before him had been made to mule, and there was nothing, absolutely nothing, anyone could do about it.

You see, Iggy beat Weecho's high score on Galaga by 12,000 points. When the news hit the streets like a Cold War air-raid siren, the homies knew Iggy's hard-fought achievement was really an act of war.

In disbelief, we all choked on our Slurpees when we heard Carlos' slobber-laden account of the play-by-play as he struggled to push each syllable through the new orthodontic retainer his mama had forbidden him to remove.

"*He what?*" we shouted. "How could anybody beat the shit outta lil' Iggy?"

We asked not because we doubted Weecho, but because we all knew he was ruthless as a blood clot in our collective nervous systems. A decorated boxer at eleven, with the slow, deliberate swagger already evident in his Nike Cortez's as they glided across elementary school playgrounds each year; he was like Montoya, the great cholo general in *American Me*—cool, heartless, and methodical. Iggy, on the other hand, was a small, ten-year-old sensitive Chicanito who collected Cabbage Patch Kids and demonstrated an early acumen for urban development when he first began constructing elaborate cities with train sets as stand-ins for trolley and subway systems in his backyard; Iggy, by eons, was the smartest kid at school, who wore glasses so large and so thick we swore he oversaw the universe while he stood perched on the community center swimming pool's diving board. Hell, Iggy's library card had even been bronzed one summer when he set an all-time record for checking out the most library books related to single-cell organisms over vacation.

2.

Pregunta: "Would you rather be a eukaryote or a protist cell?"
Respuesta: "Neither, *play-ya*, I'm bacterial!"

3.

Iggy's parents paced their front yard when it was apparent he might not make it home before sundown. Everyone knew that the sun's weakening heat on our forearms as evening approached was Iggy's requisite weekend curfew. Iggy's parents soon enlisted the neighborhood denizens to help them search the sleek, steamy, summer day streets for their mijito, avenues, according to his hyper-paranoiac parents, that would soon darken to zero-visibility when the sun set and a jungle of mosquitoes, child molesters, and chupacabras populated the darkness. It was nights like these that Iggy's mama swore she heard the yowls of distant rhesus monkeys hollering danger from the trees.

All evening a menagerie of parents, grandparents, tíos y tías, and neighbor-hood kids (although they knew the truth, but would never ever blurt a hint of it) walked behind sergeant Venegas' police car as it crawled up and down the block with Iggy's father holding a police-issued bullhorn to his mouth, yelling "Iggy, mijo, Come out! We're not mad at you! Your mom made you chilaquiles, your favorite—breakfast for dinner!" While Iggy's mom walked alongside him, convinced her lamb had been stung by a bee and lay suffering somewhere from an anaphylactic attack, her Iggy curled into a fetal position, trembling, emitting quick micro-breaths beneath a bougainvillea he used for shelter. "We need to save my boy," she cried, "bees love Iggy because his skin smells just like jamoncillo!"

4.

The search party never bothered to check 7-Eleven. It was four blocks away from Iggy's house, and Iggy was forbidden to leave his own side of the block without adult supervision. Unbeknownst to them, however, Iggy had been secretly venturing from the virtual, corrugated fence his parents had installed in his mind to hang with the boys at Bucklin Park, the New Star alley, and 7-Eleven. "Liberation never felt so great," he exclaimed one dusty afternoon while riding handlebars on Jesus' PK Ripper. "Que viva Augusto Sandino! Que viva Pancho Villa!" And in a united, color guard-timed response, the nine-boy BMX procession shouted their you're-one-of-us-now-grito: "Y que viva Iggy Iggs!"

It took Iggy two and a half weeks of clandestine trips to America's favorite neon 24-hour convenient store to shatter the Mt. Everest of adolescent feats. An achievement that would have made Che Guevara proud. As we held our collective breath and stood physiologically hopped on Caramello's, Super Big Gulps and envy, we all waited with wide-eyed anticipation for the day Iggy could finally type his initials into the dark, star-studded galactic screen that would stand securely undisturbed on a Himalayan heap of quarters for centuries. And we knew it wouldn't be long thereafter before Iggy stomped on Stephen Krogman's 15,999,990 point world record. The world was changing, and Iggy was its drum major.

5.

Iggs…

6.

We received the details that filled the gaps in Carlos' initial report compliments of Leon Muñoz's death-defying recognizance mission. He secretly followed the two boys on foot from 4th street like a Viet Cong guerilla fighter, using mulberry trees and oleanders along the way to help camouflage himself in his Saturday's finest: a complete Mexican national soccer team uniform knockoff: *"Viva El Tri!"*

Leon reported back to us later that day as we huddled in an undisclosed alley listening to the bludgeoning heroics of dear Ignacio Guadalupe Hidalgo Montes. "Yo, bro," Leon assured us, "John Rambo didn't have it this bad, dude. And we all know here that he got the ass-whuppin of ass-whuppins at the hands of Captain Vinh in Rambo: First Blood Part II." A wave of head nods serpentined among the group until we all secretly thought of Rambo's beautiful Vietnamese contact, Co Bao, sly smiles subtly taking residence on every one of our brown faces.

7.

With Iggy's nose bloodied and his eyes swollen beneath his eyeglasses (apparently, Weecho had the decency to remove them before dropping a set of fiery combinations on Iggy's Bambi-brown eyes), Iggy stood at Galaga and played for hours, depositing quarters into a machine that accepted them obediently alongside Weecho's fists tightened like small sacks of flour ready to explode across Iggy's chin at the first sign of resignation. Rudolf the cashier, a.k.a. Pac Man Fever, because of his uncanny ability to catch Cheese Puffs in his mouth fired at him from a slingshot twenty yards out, did nothing to intervene. He was Weecho's older brother's homeboy and understood the importance of Machiavellian neighborhood rule. Pac Man Fever simply broke change laughingly as Weecho dropped dollar after dollar on the counter, generously footing the bill that would rewrite the annals of history.

8.

According to Leon's calculator watch, Iggy's original high score was finally surpassed and secured at 9:23 pm when Weecho shoved Iggy aside to punch in his initials, muttering *who's the real muthafucka* this and *muthafuckas need to know* that.

Standing quietly beside him, Iggy mistook the static desert moon that hung just beyond the 7-Eleven window for death's bright eye before he dropped from exhaustion and dreamt of a vast city inhabited by bees.

9.

Three months later 7-Eleven brass decided to remove Galaga, Missile Command, and the perennially leaning Bally's Flash Gordon pinball machine from the store. Pac Man Fever was fired when he got caught stealing Donruss Diamond Kings from baseball card packs and resealing them with a hot glue gun he stole from his mother, Chata. Apparently, there was a sting operation that included twenty-four-hour surveillance monitoring Pac Man Fever's whereabouts, illegal wire taps, two undercover regional managers who posed as hot wing connoisseurs, and eventually, a lie detector test that Pac Man Fever actually beat, but then blew, when he couldn't lie about his fondness for Circle K slushies, thus labeled a traitor.

Weecho moved to central California with his family after his older brother got into some trouble with the law. We heard through the lightening-quick chisme cable that Weecho would soon become a Golden Gloves champ, an accomplishment that would lead him to a successful amateur boxing career. He nearly made the Olympics. Though his brother got life, Weecho excelled and became a standout community member in his new town when he began a nonprofit that supported formerly incarcerated men re-entering society.

As for Iggy, he vowed never to play video games again. When Nintendo launched its world-wide home invasion, he sat cross-legged outside KB Toys in white pants, a white T-shirt with a Star Trek Iron On patch, and a white hoodie like some Trappist monk warning of a future that banished marbles, cardio and the infinite possibilities of the analog imagination.

Acknowledgments

I am grateful to Futurepoem's Carly Dashiell, Dan Machlin, Aiden Farrell, and Ariel Yelen. Your support, kindness, and vision are infectious.

I am also deeply thankful to Futurepoem Guest Editors Rosa Alcalá, Marie Buck, and Farnoosh Fathi. I am still floored that you saw something in this manuscript. I am a fan of your respective works, which makes this journey extra special.

Many thanks to Carmen Giménez, Tim Z. Hernández, Sawako Nakayasu, and Roberto Tejada. With admiration and appreciation. My goodness.

Thanks also to Laurie Ann Guerrero.

Big thanks to Marcella Durand, HR Hegnauer, and Tom of Everything Studio.

I would like to thank the following magazines, and their editors, for their support and generosity: *Columbia Review*, *The Fairy Tale Review*, *Hotel Amerika*, *New American Writing*, *Puerto del Sol*, and *The Rumpus*.

To my parents, Manuel and Margaret, always.

For Javiercito, our little light and fortune.

And for Luka, the giant talk, our wonder-maker.

Nerve Curriculum is also dedicated to Jimmie Cannon (1929-2009) and Carmelle Kuehn. High school jazz and creative writing teachers, whose senior-year interventions made all of the difference.

¡Mil gracias!

References

Harvey, PJ. "In the Dark Places." *Let England Shake*. Island Records, 2011.

Hirschman, Jack. "Mother." *Front Lines*. City Lights, 2002.

Hurston, Zora Neale, and Edwidge Danticat. *Their Eyes Were Watching God*. HarperCollins Publishers, 2021.

Kim, Hyesoon, and Don Mee Choi. "Ghost School." *Sorrowtoothpaste Mirrorcream*. Action Books, 2014.

Koch, Kenneth. "At Extremes." *A Possible World: Poems*. A.A. Knopf, 2004.

Olivarez, José. "Rumors." *Citizen Illegal*. Haymarket Books, 2019.

Wikipedia riff on p. 12 based on: "Age of Towns Scheme." Wikipedia Foundation. en.wikipedia.org/wiki/town.

Yau, John. "A Painter's Formulas, An Alchemist's Notes, and an Unknown Convict's Ravings Found on a Blacke Calendar." *Bijoux in the Dark*. Letter Machine Editions, 2018.

This first edition, first printing, includes 26 limited edition copies signed by the author and lettered a-z.